Beco's Big Year

A Baby Elephant Turns One

By Linda Stanek

COLUMBUS
ZOO®
AND AQUARIUM

This publication has been made possible through the generous funding of the Frances J. Coultrap Endowment at the Columbus Zoo and Aquarium.

To my grandmother, Dale Minshall, who taught me, through example, what gratitude is.

Text copyright © 2010 by Linda Stanek

Front cover photo copyright © 2009 Grahm Jones/Columbus Zoo and Aquarium
Back cover photo copyright © 2009 Tom Dodge/The Columbus Dispatch

Publisher's Cataloging-In-Publication Data
(Prepared by The Donohue Group, Inc.)
   Stanek, Linda.   Beco's big year : a baby elephant turns one / by Linda Stanek.
      p. : ill. ; cm.
   Summary: Celebrates and chronicles the surprise birth and endearing milestones of Beco, a baby Asian
elephant, born at the Columbus Zoo and Aquarium in Columbus, Ohio. Beco learns to swim, use his trunk,
play with toys and follow directions, all under the watchful eye of his mother, Phoebe. Also included is
information about baby elephants, how elephants are taken care of at the zoo, and a section on elephant
conservation.
   Interest age level: 8 and up.

   ISBN: 978-0-9841554-2-2 (hardcover)
   ISBN: 978-0-9841554-3-9 (pbk.)

1. Beco (Elephant)–Juvenile literature. 2. Phoebe (Elephant)–Juvenile literature. 3. Elephants–Infancy–
Juvenile literature. 4. Elephants–Conservation–Juvenile literature. 5. Captive elephants–Juvenile
literature. 6. Columbus Zoo--Juvenile literature. 7. Beco (Elephant) 8. Phoebe (Elephant) 9. Elephants–
Infancy. 10. Elephants–Conservation. 11. Captive elephants. 12. Columbus Zoo. I. Title.
QL737.P98 S73 2010
599.676

Published by Columbus
Zoological Park Association
9990 Riverside Drive
Powell, OH 43065
www.columbuszoo.org

Produced for the Columbus
Zoological Park Association by
School Street Media
info@schoolstreetmedia.com
www.schoolstreetmedia.com

Printed in the United States of America

2 4 6 8 10 9 7 5 3 1

Foreword

Who doesn't love babies? And who doesn't love elephants? Combine the two, and you end up with a powerful tug on the heartstrings! *Beco's Big Year* by Linda Stanek will give you some insight into one of the many special treats we get to enjoy every day at the zoo—Beco, the baby elephant.

In reading this book, you'll get a rare "behind the scenes" peek at Beco's world. You'll meet the other elephants that live at the zoo, including Phoebe, Beco's loving and protective mom. You'll learn how Beco learns: what food is good to eat, how to drink water, and which toys are the most fun! You will see what Beco's human companions do every day to make sure that he is healthy and happy.

Both Asian and African elephants are in great danger in the wild. The Columbus Zoo and Aquarium supports a number of conservation and research projects that are designed to improve the outlook for elephants everywhere. As human populations grow larger, it seems that the risk for elephants grows larger, too. To reduce those risks for elephants, in fact for all wildlife, and insure that they continue to be a part of our world, we need to make sure that people care about them. We know that introducing people to elephants during a visit to the zoo is a great way to get that done. We hope that this book will accomplish the same thing!

—Jack Hanna

Director Emeritus
of the Columbus Zoo
and Aquarium

Exciting News!

For almost two years, the people at the Columbus Zoo watch and wait. An Asian elephant named Phoebe gets bigger and bigger and bigger.

Animal doctors, called vets, have great news. Phoebe is going to have a baby! Before, she weighed 6,800 pounds. As her baby grows, Phoebe gains more than a thousand pounds. Now, she is up to almost 8,000 pounds.

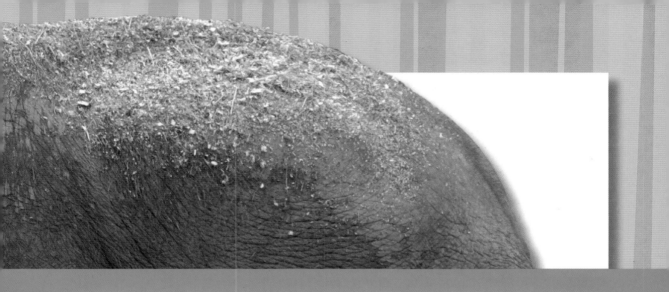

Know Your Elephants

The two main elephant species are the African elephant and the Asian elephant.[1] Just by their names, you can tell where they live: Africa and Asia. You can tell them apart in several ways.

African elephants
(Loxodonta africana)

- larger: up to 11 feet tall and 14,000 pounds
- huge, fanlike ears
- smooth forehead
- males and females grow tusks
- two "fingers" at the tip of their trunks
- listed as a "threatened" species

Asian elephants
(Elephas maximus)

- smaller: up to 10 feet tall and 12,000 pounds
- smaller ears
- two bumps on the forehead
- a hump at the shoulder
- males grow tusks; females grow small "tushes"
- one "finger" at the tip of their trunks
- listed as an "endangered" species

[1]DNA studies in 2004 prove that the African forest elephant *(Loxodonta cyclotis)* is a third species.

One day, her tests show something exciting. Phoebe will have her baby in the next few days.

The elephant keepers, called handlers, know that most elephant babies are born at night. They make sure someone is around to watch Phoebe all night long. They want to be close by when the baby is born.

Who's Who at the Zoo

Handlers

Handlers are the people who spend the most time with the elephants. They watch over them, feed them, bathe them, train them, and generally care for them. The elephants learn to trust their handlers over time. This trusting relationship makes it possible for humans to work with these huge animals. Without handlers, zoos would not be able to have elephants. Handlers always work in pairs, because sometimes two hands are just not enough.

Veterinarians

Often called "vets," these men and women are animal doctors. They don't work with the elephants on a daily basis, but they do perform all the necessary medical care as it's needed. They also help the handlers figure out what nutritional changes are necessary to keep the elephants in the best health.

A Baby Elephant Is Born!

Phoebe surprises everyone two days later. Her baby, called a calf, is born outside in the middle of the day! Handlers rush to the outdoor yard. They find

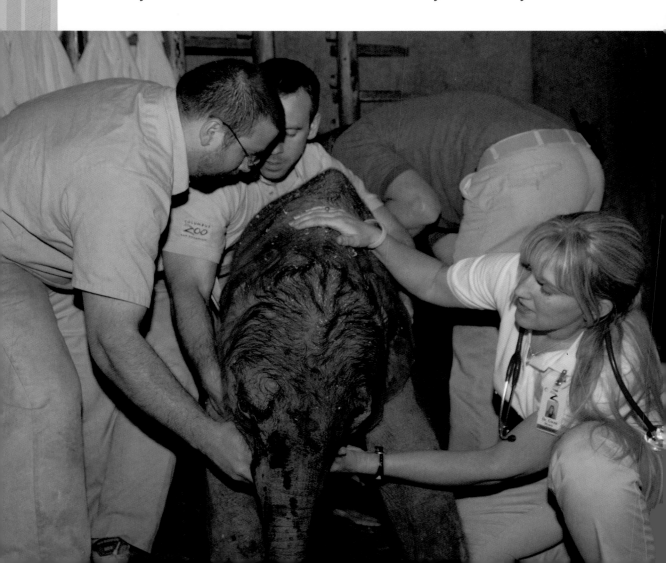

the little elephant lying on the ground. It's a boy! Both mother and baby seem okay. What a relief!

But there is a problem. The new calf was born far from the elephant building. It will be cold tonight, so the baby must be moved indoors. The handlers wonder how they'll get the little guy inside. Even though he is a tiny elephant, at over 300 pounds, he's too heavy to carry. The ground is wet and slippery. Can the little elephant walk that far? After all, he's just been born.

A "Birth" Day Surprise

"Having a baby elephant born is a very big deal," says veterinarian Gwen Myers. "For almost two years, we planned for delivering this baby. We had our supplies ready, and we had planned who would do what, when." They were expecting all of this to happen inside and at night. But Phoebe must not have known about their plans, because she had her baby outdoors during the day.

It is very rare for an elephant to be born during the day. In fact, sometimes a daytime delivery can mean something is wrong with the mother or baby. The zoo's handlers worried about that as they rushed to Phoebe.

Handler Aaron Kazmierczak was the first to see the elephant calf. "He was lying on his side, almost like he was asleep. Phoebe was walking around him, already checking him out. And he was moving, so I knew he was okay," Aaron says.

Getting Them Inside

In only thirty minutes, the little guy is on his feet. He's about as tall as his handlers' hips. The workers wait for him to get his balance.

Handlers put a strap under the calf's belly so they can hold him steady as he walks. Another handler leads Phoebe toward the barn. Her newborn tries to stay with her. They all move slowly toward the building. Then the baby elephant slips and falls! The vets hold their breath and watch. The calf gets back up and continues on wobbly legs.

Beco's Check-up

Once indoors, vets check the calf. They look at his skin, his eyes, and even inside his mouth. They take blood. The newborn calf looks perfect. By bedtime that night, he is drinking his mother's milk. He'll drink three gallons and gain three pounds each day.

It's been a good start for the baby elephant. Still, the handlers will stay close for the next few weeks. They'll even sleep near Phoebe's stall at night. It is good to keep a close eye on him for a while.

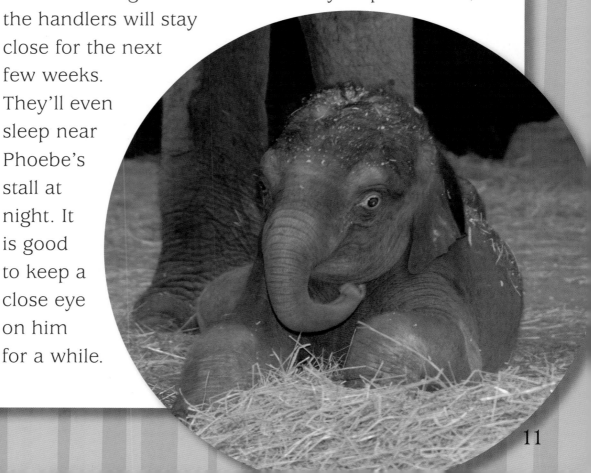

Baby's First Days

For the first two days, the baby and his mom stay inside in their stall. Visitors want to see the new baby, but handlers know he needs time to get used to his new home.

Home Sweet Home

The elephants at the Columbus Zoo live in a big, heated building. It has eleven stalls, an area with showers, a place for toys, and a giant room—bigger than two basketball courts—called a community room.

The community room is where the elephants spend time with each other. It has huge, glass windows so visitors outside the room can watch them.

At night, the elephants sleep together in the community room, or they sleep in their stalls. When elephants spend the night in the community room, they can go through doors to their outside yard to take an evening stroll or sleep under the stars.

Head keeper, Adam Felts says, "We know where each of them sleeps, because when they lie down, all the wood chips and hay on their backs fall off, forming elephant angels (like snow angels), and it is obvious who is who."

Getting a Drink

When he's three days old, the little calf watches his mom drink from a hose. She scoops water into her trunk and lifts it to her mouth. Her baby tries it, and—surprise!—he gets a drink, too. The handlers are amazed, because this little guy has learned to drink water so soon.

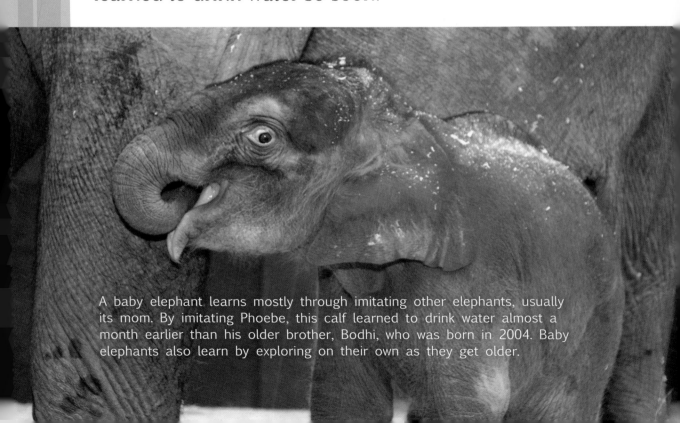

A baby elephant learns mostly through imitating other elephants, usually its mom. By imitating Phoebe, this calf learned to drink water almost a month earlier than his older brother, Bodhi, who was born in 2004. Baby elephants also learn by exploring on their own as they get older.

The Baby Gets a Name!

When the baby elephant is one week old, the zoo begins a contest to name him. People submit names at the zoo or on the zoo's Web site. For seventeen days, the staff collects names. More than 11,000 are submitted.

A panel of judges narrows down the choices to four: Sattva, Damai, Siddhartha, and Beco. The name Beco is a combination of this mother's name, Phoebe, and his father's name, Coco.

Fans of the zoo get to vote again. Out of more than 12,000 votes, nearly half go to the winning name. Zoo officials announce his name on Mother's Day, May 10, 2009. Beco it is!

Outside at Last!

After two weeks, handlers take Phoebe and Beco out to the yard where he was born. He stays close to his mom, walking under her belly or standing between her legs. Now and then, Beco is brave enough to dart out to look around. Then a new sight or smell makes him nervous, and he runs back under his mom.

As Beco gets older, he leaves his mother's side more often. A bird lands on the ground between Beco and Phoebe. Beco's ears go out, a sign that he's worried. He edges carefully around the bird, and then runs back to safety.

When Phoebe walks behind a boulder, Beco looks up and can't see her. His ears go out. Then he stands still and bellows! Phoebe comes running to her baby.

Mom and Baby

Beco and his mom spend time every day in the community room. There, visitors can watch them through the big windows. Many days, Beco falls asleep right between his mom's front feet. Phoebe drops hay as she chews, and it lands on Beco. At times, it covers him completely, turning him into a little hay pile. When Phoebe wants the hay that's under Beco, she scoots him to one side with her foot. But it doesn't wake the sleeping calf.

Fun in the Mud

Elephants love mud. It protects their skin from bugs and the sun. One day in the yard, Phoebe goes to the mud hole. She grabs a bit of mud and tries to fling it onto herself. But she misses, and the mud goes straight into Beco's eye. The calf squints and runs to his handlers as if to say, "Help me!"

After that, Beco runs to the handlers every time his mom goes to the mud hole. One day Phoebe is away from the mud hole, and Beco goes to look at it. He gets close and—oops! In he slides, just a bit, and he makes a great discovery. Mud isn't so bad when it's on your feet!

Handlers As Helpers

It is natural for mother Asian elephants to have other elephants as helpers. Recently, scientists have found that in the wild females live in groups of four to eight. When one elephant has a baby, the others help watch over and care for it. So it may seem natural to Phoebe to have her handlers close by to help take care of Beco.

"Though we aren't elephants, we consider ourselves to be somewhat a part of her peer group," says Adam Felts, one of Phoebe's handlers.

Beco's Blue Boomerball

One day, the handlers bring Beco a big, blue ball. Phoebe doesn't play with it, so Beco ignores it, too. The handlers call Beco to them as they stand by the ball. They praise and pet Beco when he touches it. They nudge the ball so it touches him, and then praise him again. Finally, Beco nudges the ball to the handlers. They cheer him on and step backwards. A game begins! Beco chases the handlers with the ball.

But Phoebe is not a fan of the ball. When the handlers leave, she pulls the calf away from the ball.

At first, Beco leaves it alone. He seems to want to please his mom. But Beco loves his ball, too, so he returns to it over and over. After two weeks, his mom gives up and lets him play with it, with the handlers or alone.

At least most of the time.

Beco's Favorites

Every kid has a few favorite toys and games, and Beco is no exception. Along with his big blue ball, Beco loves to grab hay out of little holes punched in a barrel. He loves to "skateboard," pushing across the ground with his back feet while his front feet are on a flattened barrel or even a layer of hay.

Do you know what else Beco loves? Getting scratched on the roof of his mouth. He lifts his trunk and tips back his head. It's almost as if he's saying, "Ah . . . that's just the spot!"

Eating Like a Big Boy

Early on, Beco plays with his mom's food. He runs through her grain. He munches on her hay. He chews on her treats, called monkey biscuits. Since he's eating bits of solid foods, the handlers decide to use apple slices to reward him while training. Food rewards tell Beco when he does the right thing. As he grows bigger, they give him monkey biscuits, too.

What in the World Is a Monkey Biscuit?

Monkey biscuits are hard, dry, dark brown biscuits, shaped like a big, fat X. They are made of corn, wheat, and soy, and handlers use them as treats for the elephants. So why aren't they called "elephant biscuits"? You guessed it! They were developed for monkeys first, but they're healthy for elephants, who love them, too.

On Today's Menu

Beco will drink his mother's milk for two full years. As he grows, he'll eat more and more solid foods, too. In the wild, full-grown Asian elephants eat up to 400 pounds of plant material a day. At the zoo, adult elephants eat four to eight bales of hay, five quarts of grain, plus vitamins and minerals each day. Adult elephants drink 25 to 30 gallons of water each day. It costs the Columbus Zoo and Aquarium about $12,000 a year to feed one adult elephant.

Beco Goes for a Swim

There's a deep pool in the elephant yard. At first, little Beco puts his feet in the shallow end, but doesn't go in. When he's four-and-a-half months old, he splashes into the deep water. Phoebe hurries to be with him. She stands on her hind legs and tries to grab him with her front legs. Beco swims in circles around her, too fast to catch.

The next few times Beco goes in the water, his mom catches him. She dunks him under and then lifts him back up. It's as if she's saying, "This is what it's like to go under," and "this is what it's like to come back up."

Swimming Lessons from Phoebe

A few years ago, Phoebe gave birth to Beco's older brother, Bodhi. One day, handlers watched something amazing happen. Phoebe went into the water with Bodhi and "taught" him to swim. She stood in the deep water on her hind legs and grabbed him with her front legs. She dunked him under, then lifted him up again. She did this over and over as she pivoted in a circle.

"It's clear, watching the video of Phoebe and Bodhi," says elephant expert and curator Harry Peachey, "as well as what we saw with Beco and have seen in other elephants, that her intent is to teach her babies to swim."

Phoebe might have been surprised that little Beco could swim so well and so fast without her help. But she "taught" him later—just to be sure.

Learning All the Time

Elephants are big and strong. Like all wild animals, they can be dangerous. To keep handlers and vets safe, zoo elephants need to be trained.

Beco's training begins when he is very young. The handlers ask him to do something. When he does it, even if it's by accident, they praise and scratch him. That lets him know he did the right thing.

The handlers ask Phoebe to stand aside so they can work with her baby. Soon Beco knows how to walk next to them. Then he learns to walk forward, walk backward, turn left, and turn right on cue. And that's just the beginning. Beco will keep learning over the next few years.

Super Mom

From the start, Phoebe allowed the handlers to do all they needed to do to keep her baby safe and healthy. She watches over him day and night, but also steps aside to let the handlers work with him alone when they need to.

Over the past year, there have been times when the young elephant got too rough with his handler. When that happens, the handler warns, "Be careful." Phoebe, understanding what the handler means, gently pulls her calf away. "She deserves a lot of credit," handler Adam Felts says with a proud smile. "She's a good mom, and we have a great relationship with her."

Working with a Target

As Beco grows older, he trains with a target. The target is a tennis ball that is screwed to the end of a wooden stick. It looks like an over-sized magic wand. In the beginning, the handlers give Beco a treat every time they touch him with the target. He learns that when he touches the target, he gets a treat. Later, Beco will come to understand that he can win treats by touching the target himself. This will help handlers get him to move to a specific place, lift a specific foot, and other helpful movements. It's a tool that the handlers use with all the elephants.

Do You Speak Elephant?

Only the handlers speak to the elephants. Elephants are taught to listen only to their handlers. Other people who have contact with them—even vets—must respect that rule.

Years ago, a variety of training words were used by different handlers to mean the same thing. There was no standard "training vocabulary" for elephants. Then, handlers decided it would be better to use the same training words for elephants everywhere. Today a standard "elephant language" is used. That way, when an elephant is moved from one zoo to another, it still understands what the new handlers are saying.

Here are some universal training words and their meanings:

- "forward"—move ahead
- "back"—move backward
- "left"—move to the left
- "right"—move to the right
- "stand"—stop moving and have all four feet on the ground
- "down"—lie down on your stomach
- "over"—roll to one side
- "up"—get up on your feet
- "trunk"—move your trunk up and out of the way
- "open"—open your mouth
- "drop it"—drop, or do not pick up, an object
- "drink"—drink from a hose
- "thank you"—a release that tells the elephant it is finished with the last request

Beco's First Bath

Elephants love water. From the time Beco is born, he is rinsed with warm water and rubbed with mineral oil to keep his skin moist. When he is six months old, he gets his first full bath. He'll have baths two or three times a week for the rest of his life.

Now that he knows how to lie down on his right or left sides on request, handlers can spray him with water, soap him up, scrub him with a big brush, and then rinse him off. It's good for his skin. And Beco loves it.

Trunks and Teeth

Beco is growing up fast! At first, he has trouble controlling his trunk. Then he learns to wrap it around things to move or lift them. Next, he practices working the tip of his trunk. He uses it like a finger to hold and pick things up.

Around the age of eight months—and because he's a boy—Beco shows signs of growing tusks. As his tusks grow in, they are checked often. After the tusks are completely grown, handlers will file them down to keep them healthy. The handlers feel inside Beco's mouth every day so he will get used to people touching him there.

That Amazing Thing Called a Trunk

An elephant's trunk is a multipurpose tool. It's used to breathe, smell, trumpet, drink, and grab things. It is strong enough to take down trees and agile enough to pick up a single piece of straw. Think about this: The entire human body has 700 muscles in it. An elephant's trunk alone has between 50,000 and 100,000 muscles! No one knows the exact number.

Elephant Teeth

Elephant tusks are super-long teeth, called incisors. At the zoo, the bulls' tusks are trimmed. This helps the tusks grow fat and strong, preventing them from breaking. It also protects the female elephants from injury when the elephants are together. Handlers trim three inches off the bulls' tusks two times a year.

Many female Asian elephants grow small tusks, called tushes. Often they are so small they don't protrude past the skin that surrounds them. Occasionally, a female will grow tushes six to eight inches long. They generally grow so slowly that the elephant might need to have them trimmed only two or three times in her lifetime.

Elephants also have four molars in their mouths. Each is the size of a brick and weighs eleven pounds. Elephant molars do not come in vertically like peoples' do. They move horizontally in the mouth, conveyor-belt-style. As one molar wears down, breaks, and falls out, another one moves into its place.

When elephants get old, and their last molars are worn, they can only eat very soft food. In the wild, they often find a marshy area to live. The marsh plants are wet and soft. As time goes on, even the marsh plants are too hard to eat and the old elephants die of starvation. Finding groups of dead elephants in these marshy areas led to the myth that there are "elephant graveyards"—specific places where elephants go to die. In truth, the elephants probably ended up there because the place provided them with food they could still eat.

Staying Healthy

As winter sets in, Beco learns to have his blood drawn. As he gets older, his blood will be checked every week to make sure he is healthy. Handlers teach Beco to stand still as a vet feels his leg. When Beco is comfortable with that, the vet sticks him with a needle. It doesn't hurt much, certainly not as much as when a person gets a shot. His handlers reassure him that everything is okay, and Beco stays calm. Because they have worked with Beco slowly and carefully, he is never frightened.

Like all animals, elephants can get sick. One type of virus can kill an elephant in a matter of days, often before handlers even know the elephant is ill. An elephant can simply be walking along, and then fall down dead. Because of this, zoo elephants get their blood tested once a week. That way, if they get the virus, vets will know in time to give them the medicine they need to save them.

Turning on Cue

In January, Beco learns to turn. He stands facing his handlers. Then, when asked to, he turns until his tail faces them. He lifts his back feet so they can be checked. Then he turns the rest of the way around to face his handlers again. Bravo, Beco!

Snow Day!

Something new comes along with the winter's chill—snow! Beco goes out into it for the very first time. He smells the snow with his trunk. He grabs some with his trunk and puts it into his mouth. It's not like anything he's ever felt before, and Beco gets excited. He plays in it—digging, running, slipping, and sliding, before returning to the elephant building to dry off and get warm.

Beco's dad, Coco, doesn't mind the snow one bit!

Hot, Cold, or In Between

Wild Asian elephants live in tropical areas with warm to hot temperatures. At the zoo, the elephants decide whether to stay in or go out as long as the temperature outside is 35 degrees or above. Colder than that, and the handlers decide if it's warm enough based on what is happening with the wind, sun, and rain. All the adult elephants in Columbus have, at one time or another, chosen to go outside to play in the snow!

Beco's 1st Birthday!

On Beco's birthday, the zoo holds a party for him. Visitors flock to celebrate. At around 1,400 pounds, Beco now weighs almost as much as five newborn elephants. He will keep growing until he's in his twenties. By then he might weigh the same as his dad, 12,000 pounds. That's more than three Volkswagen Beetles. He could be ten feet tall, as high as a basketball hoop. But for now he's still a baby, learning and growing every day. And for zoo visitors, the handlers, the vets, Phoebe, and Beco, it's been a big year!

Beco's birthday cake is made of ice.

Beco's Big Year

The Need for Elephant Conservation

Elephants all over the world are in danger of becoming extinct. Asian elephants are even rarer than their larger relative, the African elephant. Once there were roughly a million elephants in Asia. Today there are only 35,000. That might sound like a lot of elephants, but with the number dropping all the time, scientists worry that they might become extinct. The Columbus Zoo and Aquarium and the Association of Zoos and Aquariums (AZA) are working to make sure elephants are with us for many, many years to come.

Keystone Animals

Elephants are more than just great animals that are in danger of becoming extinct. Elephants are considered a "keystone" animal—the survival of many other species depends on the survival of elephants. How does the survival of elephants affect the lives of other animals?

First of all, elephants help to create the habitats that other animals depend on to survive. One of the ways they do this, for example, is that elephants tear down trees, which opens space for the growth of grasslands. They also eat and partially digest certain tree seeds with very thick coverings. The seeds inside cannot grow unless they have passed through the digestive tract of an elephant. The seeds end up in

elephant dung, which acts as fertilizer to help these trees spout. As time goes by, elephants create forests where there had been grassland and create grassland where there had been forest.

This rotation of plant life helps the soil stay rich and fertile, and that helps wild animals overall. If elephants became extinct, those trees with extra-thick seedpods would also become extinct. Then the small animals that depend on those trees would become extinct. And the next step would be that the larger predators—perhaps a jungle cat—would not have enough prey, and they could become extinct, as well. As you can see, the cycle of extinction has long-reaching effects.

What Can a Zoo Do?

For more than twenty years, the Columbus Zoo and Aquarium has been working to support elephant conservation. One of the zoo's goals is to create a sustainable population of elephants in North America. That means the zoos would have enough living elephants that are having babies that the species would never become extinct. It's even possible that one day some of these North American elephants could be used to improve populations in the wild.

But the zoo's work extends beyond Columbus, or even North America. The Columbus Zoo constantly works with scientists around the world. Sometimes findings from research done in the wild is tested and even furthered by scientists in zoos. Other times, knowledge gained at zoos is passed on and used to help elephants in the wild. This sharing of research and information is a vital link in the effort to keep these animals alive.

The Columbus Zoo funds research projects to learn more about elephants and shares the information with people in other countries. They fund veterinarian research, training, and support (including providing medicines and medical equipment), as well as funding electronic equipment such as GPS collars and radios to track elephants. The zoo funds projects focused on reducing conflict between humans and elephants. One such project plans "corridors" of wild areas for elephant migration, so they won't pass through and damage the crops and plantations of local people.

Beco Has a Mission

Beco and his North American relatives provide scientists with a wealth of information about their species. These amazing animals have another very important mission, too—to help the public understand and care about them. Research shows that seeing a live elephant has a much greater impact on people than seeing one on television. And when people care about an animal, they are more interested in participating in conservation efforts that, in the end, benefit us all.

Recommended Reading

For ages 4-8

Arnold, Katya. *Elephants Can Paint Too!* New York: Atheneum, 2005.

Butler, John. *Bashi, Elephant Baby*. Viking Kestrel Picture Books. New York: Viking Juvenile, 1998.

Clarke, Ginjer L. *Baby Elephant*. All Aboard Science Reader. New York: Grosset & Dunlap, 2009.

Davies, Kate. *Elephants*. Usborne First Reading. Tulsa, Oklahoma: Educational Development Corporation, 2009.

DK Publishing *Elephant*. Watch Me Grow Series. New York: DK Publishing, 2005.

Dorros, Arthur. *Elephant Families*. Let's-Read-and-Find-Out Science 2. New York: HarperCollins, 1994.

Knudsen, Shannon. *African Elephants*. Pull Ahead Books. Minneapolis: Lerner Publications, 2006.

Laiz, Jana. *Elephants of the Tsunami*. North Egremont, Massachusetts: EarthBound Books, 2007.

May, Paul. *Elephants: Wild Reads*. New York: Oxford University Press, 2009.

For ages 9-12

Anderson, Jill. *Elephants*. Wild Ones Series. Minnetonka, Minnesota: NorthWord Books for Young Readers, 2006.

Firestone, Mary. *Top 50 Reasons to Care About Elephants: Animals in Peril*. Berkeley Heights, New Jersey: Enslow Publishers, 2010.

Gish, Melissa. *Elephants*. Living Wild Series. Mankato, Minnesota: Creative Education, 2009.

Joubert, Dereck. *Face to Face with Elephants*. Face to Face With Animals Series. Des Moines, Iowa: National Geographic Children's Books, 2008.

Kalman, Bobbie. *Endangered Elephants*. Earth's Endangered Animals Series. New York: Crabtree Publishing Company, 2005.

Lockwood, Sophie. *Elephants*. The World of Mammals Series. Mankato, Minnesota: Child's World, 2008.

Morgan, Jody. *Elephant Rescue: Changing the Future for Endangered Wildlife*. Firefly Animal Rescue Series. Richmond Hill, Ontario: Firefly Books, 2004.

Redmond, Ian. *Eyewitness: Elephant*. New York: DK Children, 2000.

Schwabacher, Martin. *Elephants*. Animals, Animals Series. Tarrytown, New York: Marshall Cavendish Children's Books, 2000.

Spilsbury, Richard. *Asian Elephant*. Heinemann First Library. Chicago: Heinemann-Raintree, 2005.

Turner, Matt. *Asian Elephant*. Animals Under Threat Series. Chicago: Heinemann-Raintree, 2005.

Wexo, John Bonnett. *Elephants*. Zoobooks Series. Peru, Illinois: Wildlife Education, Ltd., 2002.

Bibliography

Interviews

Barrie, Dr. Michael, DVM. Director of Animal Health, Columbus Zoo and Aquarium. Interview. November 3, 2009.

Davis, Matt, Keeper. Columbus Zoo and Aquarium. Interview. November 9, 2009.

Felts, Adam. Head keeper for the Mainland Asia Region, Columbus Zoo and Aquarium. Interview. November 9, 2009.

Kazmierczak, Aaron. Keeper. Columbus Zoo and Aquarium. Interview. November 9, 2009.

Meyer, Dr. Gwen, DVM. Veterinarian. Columbus Zoo and Aquarium. Interview. November 4, 2009.

Peachey, Harry. Curator for the Mainland Asia Region. Columbus Zoo and Aquarium. Interviews. November 4, 2009 and January 17, 2010.

Articles

Butcher, Bonnie. "Zoo asks public to pick name for new elephant." *This Week*. April 9, 2009.

"Columbus Zoo Baby Elephant Debuts Friday—Naming Contest Announced." www.columbuszoo.org. April 2, 2009.

"Columbus Zoo Baby Elephant Napping and Nursing." www.columbuszoo.org. March 28, 2009.

"Columbus Zoo elephant ready to give birth." United Press International. March 2, 2009.

"Columbus Zoo Trumpets News of Elephant Birth." Reuters. March 27, 2009.

Gray, Kathy Lynn. "Beco the elephant: Babies, sigh. They grow so fast." Columbus Dispatch. September 27,2009.

Gray, Kathy Lynn. "Zoo trumpeting its newest arrival." *Columbus Dispatch*. March 28, 2009.

Lane, Mary Beth. "Zoo's baby elephant has a name: Beco." *Columbus Dispatch*. May 11, 2009.

"Mammals: Elephant." San Diego Zoo's *Animal Bytes*. November 8, 2009

Photo Credits

COLUMBUS
ZOO
AND AQUARIUM

Mission Statement

We exist to enrich our community's quality of life and to inspire a greater appreciation of wildlife for the advancement of conservation action.

About the Columbus Zoo and Aquarium

Founded in 1927, the Columbus Zoo and Aquarium gained international recognition and stature with the 1956 birth of Colo, the world's first zoo-born gorilla. Today, the Zoo is a nationally and internationally acclaimed conservation center, housing more than 700 species, including 37 endangered and threatened species. Annually, the Zoo supports more than 70 wildlife conservation projects around the world through its Conservation Fund and Partners in Conservation.

In addition to its role as a global conservation leader, the Columbus Zoo and Aquarium is a renowned year-round education and recreation facility for visitors of all ages, backgrounds, and experiences. Each year, the Zoo attracts more than 1.8 million visitors, educates more than 250,000 children and adults, and serves as a field trip destination for more than 130,000 students. The Zoo resides on 580 acres, making it one of the fastest-growing zoos in the world and the third-largest municipally affiliated zoo in North America.

The Columbus Zoo and Aquarium is an Association of Zoo and Aquariums (AZA) accredited institution, which requires member organizations to adhere to high standards in animal care and demonstrate strong programs in conservation, research, and education.

Acknowledgements

I'd like to express my gratitude to the many people at the Columbus Zoo and Aquarium who were instrumental in creating this book: elephant expert and curator, Harry Peachey, for the knowledge he so willingly shared with me; Head keeper and handler, Adam Felts, whose personal narratives made this story come alive for me, and for his tolerance for my innumerable emails and requests; Veterinarians Mike Barrie and Gwen Myers who shared with me the medical side, complete with the joys and anxieties of having a baby elephant born under their care; and keepers and handlers, Matt Davis and Aaron Kazmierczak, both of whom played vital roles in Beco's growth. Your stories have captivated me. Your dedication to the species and love for Beco and Phoebe is truly heartwarming. The work you all do to better understand, provide for, and protect this amazing endangered species is a gift to us all.

Thanks also to my writing group—those five talented, tenacious women who have been with me for more than six years as we've grown together in writing strength and success. Jen, Chrissie, Mary Beth, Linda, and Dale, your tough critiques and unwavering encouragement have made writing with you a challenge and a joy.

My thanks also to my editor and friend Tanya Dean Anderson for working her magic on this book as she does with every book she touches. Your commitment to getting great books into the hands of children speaks directly to this teacher's heart. Thank you for your friendship, guidance, faith in my abilities and your prayers.

And finally, I want to thank Ken Blalock for his endless support, partnership, humor, and love. Through good times and bad, you are a shining light in my world.

About the Author

Linda Stanek was born and raised in Columbus, Ohio, and loved visiting the zoo as a child. She became a Columbus Zoo member when her kids were young, taking them to visit the zoo often. Raising two boys sometimes made her feel as if she lived in a zoo—with dogs, cats, rabbits, fish, and guinea pigs. They even hatched some chicks!

Today her children are grown, and she spends her time taming stray cats and corralling words into stories—both fiction and nonfiction. In addition to writing books, she writes for magazines, e-zines, and non-profit organizations. She also writes teacher's guides for award-winning children's books.

Linda has a degree in elementary education from The Ohio State University and lives in Columbus with her three cats, Frankie (named after a Columbus Crew soccer player), Chloe (just because she likes the name), and Cubby (named after the Chicago Cubs baseball team). Linda loves to visit schools and do presentations, and you can still find her at the zoo when time allows.

Beco's Big Year is her second book.